PROJECT 2025 Blueprint for a New America 

Charting a Path for Authoritarian Rule - The Heritage Foundation's Conservative Manifesto for The Next Administration. Summarized Edition.

Isaac J. Stones

INTRODUCTION

In 2023, a new initiative took shape that could dramatically alter the direction of American governance as we know it. The Heritage Foundation, a long-standing conservative think tank, quietly released a blueprint called Project 2025, crafted with the vision of reshaping the U.S. government from within. Billed as a strategic policy guide for the next conservative administration, Project 2025 outlines sweeping changes across nearly every facet of American life. What might initially seem like just another political roadmap is, upon closer inspection, a meticulously crafted manifesto with far-reaching implications for the future of American democracy.

At its core, Project 2025 seeks to consolidate executive power, reduce federal oversight, and enforce conservative policies through every level of government. The document's authors, a network of prominent conservative leaders, think tanks, and legal experts,have taken a comprehensive approach to overhaul existing systems in ways that would cement conservative influence for generations. With detailed plans for restructuring agencies, appointing ideologically aligned officials, and dismantling regulatory protections, Project 2025 marks an unprecedented effort to centralize authority within the executive branch, enabling rapid implementation of its policies without the usual checks and balances of the federal bureaucracy.

The Heritage Foundation's involvement is far from surprising. Established in the 1970s, it has long been a leader in conservative policy formation, particularly around issues such as deregulation, judicial appointments, and defense. The think tank has steadily built a reputation as a powerful ally to conservative leaders, providing research, policy suggestions, and an extensive network of loyal supporters. Yet, with Project 2025, the Heritage Foundation, in collaboration with other conservative organizations, has taken a bolder, more comprehensive step toward consolidating influence, paving the way for a brand of governance that diverges sharply from the democratic principles of separation of powers and federal oversight.

Why should this matter to the average American? Because Project 2025 could fundamentally reshape the balance of power within the United States government. It is a project aimed not only at governance but at enforcing a specific ideology, often at the expense of established democratic norms. For those concerned about the implications of unchecked executive power, curtailed rights, and decreased transparency, this blueprint represents a potential turning point. Project 2025, if fully realized, could transform the U.S. political landscape, challenging long-standing principles that define American democracy.

The stakes are high, and the questions are urgent. Will this shift in power serve the nation's interest, or will it create an environment where dissent is stifled and power is wielded unilaterally? The pages ahead explore these questions, analyzing the potential consequences of Project 2025 for America's future.

CHAPTER ONE

The Blueprint for Power Consolidation

When the Heritage Foundation unveiled Project 2025, it marked a watershed moment in American conservative politics. This document was not merely a list of policy suggestions or campaign promises; it was a comprehensive playbook for a fundamental reshaping of the U.S. government. Project 2025, unlike many past policy blueprints, was developed with one primary goal in mind: to concentrate power within the executive branch and align federal government actions strictly with a conservative agenda. Let's explore the architects and contributors of Project 2025, its organizational structure and backing, and its explicit strategies for consolidating executive power.

Key Architects and Contributors of Project 2025

Project 2025 is the brainchild of a coalition of conservative powerhouses, led by the Heritage Foundation but involving a constellation of allied think tanks, policy experts, and political leaders. The Heritage Foundation, known for its longstanding influence in conservative circles, took the lead in crafting this ambitious blueprint. Yet Heritage was far from alone in this endeavor. The project brought together influential conservative organizations such as the American Enterprise Institute (AEI), the Federalist Society, and the Claremont Institute, each of which contributed specific policy recommendations and areas of expertise.

The key figures behind Project 2025 read like a who's-who of conservative activism and thought leadership. Heritage President Kevin Roberts and his team played a central role in coordinating efforts and aligning the various contributing organizations under a unified strategy. Figures like Leonard Leo, the former vice president of the Federalist Society, whose impact on judicial appointments has already shaped the Supreme Court, offered legal and constitutional perspectives. Stephen Moore of the Committee to Unleash Prosperity lent his voice to economic policy, while Claremont's scholars, known for their focus on the "American founding principles," emphasized issues of national identity and governance structure. Together, these architects and contributors crafted a document that blends economic, legal, and ideological goals, each designed to solidify conservative influence well beyond the four-year term of a presidency.

Their collaboration underscores the strategic depth of Project 2025. Rather than merely advising a future administration, these contributors envision a political and cultural transformation rooted in conservative ideals. By bringing together a wide array of expertise, they have ensured that every facet of the federal government, be it the courts, environmental regulation, or social policy, is touched by a unified conservative vision. The contributors' collective experience in influencing policy, placing ideologically aligned judges, and crafting legislation to advance conservative ideals is, in itself, an indication of their determination to shape the future of American governance.

Structure and Organization of the Project

Project 2025's organizational structure resembles a powerful political machine designed to operate efficiently and to maximize conservative influence across federal agencies. Spearheaded by the Heritage Foundation, the project operates with a defined hierarchy that includes core policy architects, advisory groups, and strategic partnerships with influential donors. Behind Heritage's leadership, several satellite organizations and donor networks provide essential funding and support, enabling Project 2025 to not only develop its ambitious goals but also to ensure they have the resources to implement these ideas within a short time frame if a conservative administration returns to power.

Funding for Project 2025 is as substantial as it is strategic. Prominent conservative donor networks, such as the Koch network and the Bradley Foundation, play a pivotal role in financing the initiative. These donors, known for supporting conservative causes and judicial appointments, see Project 2025 as a long-term investment in shaping government policy according to conservative values. Major private donors, including wealthy individuals and family foundations with deep-rooted ties to the conservative movement, also lend financial support, ensuring that Project 2025 has the resources to influence policy far beyond the confines of a single administration.

Project 2025's supporters are not limited to private entities. Several public figures, including Republican legislators and former cabinet officials, have publicly expressed support for its goals. Their endorsements serve a dual purpose: they not only lend legitimacy to the project but also signal to the broader conservative base that this initiative is aligned with mainstream conservative values. By cultivating these alliances, Project 2025 positions itself as a well-supported, comprehensive movement, not merely a fringe project.

This combination of public and private backing also provides Project 2025 with the flexibility to operate in various spheres. It has the resources to push its agenda through lobbying, media campaigns, and grassroots mobilization. Simultaneously, it can rely on institutional support from think tanks and lawmakers who share its vision. In doing so, Project 2025 can advance its objectives both publicly and behind the scenes, ensuring that its influence extends well beyond a single election cycle.

How Project 2025 Aims to Centralize Power Within the Executive Branch

At the heart of Project 2025 lies a desire to dramatically centralize power within the executive branch, creating a government that operates swiftly and with minimal opposition. This goal represents a fundamental shift from the traditional system of checks and balances that has long defined American governance. Project 2025 seeks to reshape government operations so that, under a future conservative administration, policies can be implemented unilaterally, with as little interference as possible from Congress, the judiciary, or independent regulatory agencies.

One of the most striking strategies proposed by Project 2025 is the reclassification of federal employees under a new category called "Schedule F." Introduced initially during the Trump administration, Schedule F would allow the president to reassign or remove large numbers of federal workers, particularly those in policy-making positions, without the usual procedural protections. This reclassification would effectively make a significant portion of the federal workforce answerable directly to the president, allowing an administration to install loyalists and replace those deemed obstructive to its agenda. Under Project 2025, Schedule F would serve as a powerful tool for reshaping the federal bureaucracy to align with conservative values, undermining the traditional concept of a nonpartisan civil service.

Project 2025 also advocates for a streamlined approach to federal agency regulations. By granting the executive branch more authority to directly manage regulatory agencies such as the Environmental Protection Agency (EPA) and the Department of Health and Human Services (HHS), the project aims to reduce the influence of longstanding regulatory frameworks that protect public health, the environment, and worker rights. For example, instead of allowing these agencies to operate independently, Project 2025 envisions placing them under tighter executive control, enabling the president to expedite deregulatory policies that align with conservative economic and environmental priorities.

In practice, this consolidation of power would mean that future executive orders and policies could face fewer hurdles, enabling rapid changes across a wide range of issues, from environmental protections to healthcare regulations and labor standards. By circumventing Congress and limiting the power of federal agencies to act independently, Project 2025 seeks to empower the executive branch to implement its agenda efficiently, without enduring prolonged legislative battles or legal challenges.

An example of this power consolidation can be seen in Project 2025's stance on judicial appointments. The project advocates for an expedited process to appoint judges who align closely with conservative values, particularly within federal district courts, which hear cases that have broad implications for public policy. By appointing judges with a shared ideological perspective, a future conservative administration could ensure that its policies face fewer legal obstacles, thus reinforcing the administration's authority.

This centralization effort, in essence, redefines the relationship between the branches of government. Project 2025 envisions an executive branch that not only initiates policy but also enforces and protects it through a network of loyal appointees and strategically placed allies within the judiciary. By limiting the influence of Congress and reducing the autonomy of federal agencies, Project 2025 outlines a path for conservative governance that is streamlined, ideologically consistent, and remarkably resilient to opposition.

Project 2025's blueprint for power consolidation is ambitious and unprecedented in its scope. Through a coalition of influential conservative figures, backed by substantial financial and institutional support, this initiative lays the groundwork for a government in which executive authority is paramount. By reshaping the federal workforce, diminishing agency independence, and aligning the judiciary with its ideals, Project 2025 charts a course that could fundamentally alter the structure of American governance. As the blueprint unfolds, its implications will reach far beyond a single administration, challenging long-standing principles of democratic checks and balances and paving the way for a new era of centralized conservative power.

CHAPTER TWO

Reimagining Government Agencies and the Federal Workforce

Project 2025 doesn't merely suggest conservative policies for the federal government; it sets out to overhaul the government's very structure and operations. At the heart of this transformation is a strategy to reshape federal agencies and the workforce that drives them, an endeavor designed to infuse the entire government apparatus with a deeply conservative ideological stance. Through ambitious restructuring, Project 2025 aims to shift the priorities, goals, and, importantly, the personnel within federal agencies to align with its conservative vision. Let's explore how Project 2025 envisions the reorganization of federal agencies, the "Schedule F" initiative's potential impact on government employees, and what these changes mean for nonpartisan governance and accountability.

Plans for Restructuring and Re-Staffing Federal Agencies to Align with Conservative Ideology

To understand the scale of Project 2025's plans, imagine a government where every agency, from environmental protection to healthcare, from education to housing, is recalibrated to implement conservative policies exclusively. Project 2025 doesn't merely advocate for adjusting agency objectives or tweaking regulations; it aims to reconfigure agencies' core missions and re-staff them with individuals committed to conservative values. This vision fundamentally reshapes agencies to ensure that conservative policy is not only enacted but maintained, regardless of future administrations.

For example, consider the Environmental Protection Agency (EPA), a frequent target of conservative criticism. Under Project 2025, the EPA's focus would shift significantly away from regulating industry emissions or enforcing environmental protections. Instead, the agency would be restructured to emphasize economic development, deregulation, and even resource exploitation, positions that align with conservative values on energy independence and minimal government interference in business. Similarly, the Department of Education could see its focus shift away from public education funding and support toward policies that prioritize private schooling and homeschooling, reflecting a conservative preference for school choice and limited federal involvement in local education.

This restructuring goes beyond policy adjustments; it involves staffing these agencies with individuals who are ideologically aligned with the goals of Project 2025. The project outlines plans to recruit and appoint senior officials who not only support conservative principles but also actively work to counteract the influence of previous administrations. Imagine a Health and Human Services Department that actively reduces regulatory oversight on healthcare providers, arguing for a free-market approach, or a Department of Labor that minimizes protections for workers in the name of job creation and economic growth. These changes would fundamentally alter how these agencies serve the American people, reshaping the role of government in everyday life according to a conservative ideological lens.

The "Schedule F" Initiative and Its Potential Impacts on Federal Employees

A central pillar of Project 2025's strategy for government restructuring is the reimplementation of "Schedule F," a job classification initially proposed by the Trump administration. Schedule F is designed to transform a significant portion of the federal workforce, particularly those involved in policy-making and administration, into at-will employees who could be easily hired or fired based on their political alignment. This classification would effectively strip tens of thousands of federal employees of long-standing protections that shield them from partisan pressure and job insecurity.

To put this in perspective, federal employees in positions labeled as "Schedule F" would no longer benefit from protections typically granted to civil servants. These protections, which include due process and job stability, are in place to ensure that government employees can perform their duties without fear of political repercussions. Under Schedule F, however, these employees could be replaced if deemed ideologically misaligned with the administration's policies, giving the president unprecedented power to reshape the federal workforce rapidly.

For example, let's consider a hypothetical scenario in which a career scientist at the EPA opposes a proposed relaxation of environmental regulations, believing it to be harmful to public health. Under current protections, this scientist could voice concerns or even refuse to comply with policies they believe violate scientific integrity. But if that scientist were reclassified under Schedule F, they could be dismissed for their dissent, making way for a replacement who would support the administration's pro-deregulation agenda. This restructuring would extend across departments, with economists, policy analysts, and administrators replaced by individuals loyal to the administration's ideological stance.

The impact of Schedule F would not only be felt by current federal employees but also would create a chilling effect on anyone considering a career in public service. The idea of job security based on expertise and neutrality would be replaced by uncertainty, where allegiance to the current administration becomes paramount. This shift threatens the idea of a nonpartisan federal workforce, one of the pillars of American democracy. Schedule F would make civil servants vulnerable to political cycles, eroding institutional knowledge and undermining continuity within government agencies.

Implications for Nonpartisan Governance and Accountability

One of the cornerstones of American democracy is a nonpartisan federal workforce. The principle of nonpartisan governance ensures that federal employees, regardless of their personal beliefs, are committed to serving the public and upholding the law impartially. It's a safeguard that keeps the government balanced, resilient, and capable of operating across various political administrations. However, Project 2025's vision threatens this foundational principle, transforming government agencies into entities driven not by expertise or public interest but by ideology.

The implementation of Schedule F and the wholesale restructuring of agencies would fundamentally alter the relationship between federal agencies and the American public. Citizens have come to rely on agencies like the FDA, CDC, and EPA to act as watchdogs, upholding health, safety, and environmental standards. But under Project 2025, these agencies could become extensions of the executive branch, with loyalty to a specific ideology prioritized over objective, fact-based decision-making.

For instance, suppose a natural disaster occurs, and agencies responsible for disaster response, like FEMA, are staffed primarily by ideologically aligned individuals who lack relevant expertise. Such a restructuring could delay response times, prioritize cost-cutting over effective aid, and reduce the overall accountability of the agency to the public. In another example, if the Department of Labor becomes focused on business interests at the expense of workers, it may dismantle essential worker protections, allowing industries to prioritize profit over safety with limited repercussions.

Project 2025's restructuring plans also raise critical concerns about accountability. Currently, government agencies operate under a system of checks and balances that include oversight by Congress, compliance with established laws, and adherence to public transparency standards. By aligning agencies directly with the administration's ideology, Project 2025 reduces the effectiveness of these oversight mechanisms. Imagine the Department of Justice under an administration aligned with Project 2025 policies. The

DOJ could deprioritize investigations into issues that conflict with conservative values or pursue actions targeting political opposition, eroding public trust in the justice system's impartiality.

Another example of diminished accountability could be seen in the Department of Education, where shifting priorities toward private schooling might reduce funding for public schools without input from educators or local governments. The effect could be a gradual erosion of public education as we know it, where resources are redirected to align with the administration's ideological preferences without public recourse or debate.

This trend of reduced accountability has profound implications for American democracy. Federal agencies, when ideologically aligned, become instruments of executive power, not vehicles for public service. The voices of career professionals, who bring decades of knowledge and expertise to their roles, are drowned out by partisan appointees who may prioritize short-term ideological goals over long-term public welfare. Such a shift erodes the public's faith in government institutions, making it harder for citizens to trust that their best interests are being represented and protected.

Project 2025's plans for restructuring federal agencies and re-staffing the workforce represent a profound shift toward ideological governance. Through initiatives like Schedule F, the project envisions a government where loyalty to conservative values outweighs expertise, institutional memory, or public accountability. The implications are clear: a government that serves as an instrument of political power rather than a guardian of public interest. In a Project 2025-aligned government, nonpartisan governance would be replaced with a machine dedicated to enforcing a single ideology, and the effects would reverberate throughout American society, affecting policy on everything from environmental protection to civil rights.

As we move forward in exploring Project 2025, this chapter serves as a reminder of the stakes involved. The reimagining of government agencies and the federal workforce would set the stage for an administration that operates with minimal opposition, a consolidated power structure that diminishes dissent and accountability. These changes would be not only structural but cultural, reshaping the very ethos of public service and introducing a new, ideologically driven era of American governance.

CHAPTER THREE

Rolling Back Regulatory Protections

At the core of Project 2025 lies a commitment to dismantling decades of regulatory protections across various domains. These rollbacks represent not only a philosophical shift toward minimal government intervention but also a profound reimagining of how industries interact with the environment, consumers, and workers. Through targeted deregulation, Project 2025 aims to streamline government, eliminating rules and restrictions that it argues stifle innovation and economic growth. Yet, these changes have far-reaching implications for the well-being of everyday Americans and the broader global community, particularly in the areas of environmental policy, consumer protections, and labor rights.

Environmental Deregulation

The most visible and impactful area of deregulation under Project 2025 is the environment, particularly in how the government manages energy policy, climate action, and natural resources. Project 2025's proponents argue that current environmental regulations hinder economic growth and American energy independence. To combat this, they propose lifting restrictions on fossil fuel extraction, reducing the EPA's enforcement authority, and scaling back government commitments to climate change initiatives. In their view, allowing industries freer access to oil, gas, and coal resources would fuel economic growth, lower energy prices, and ensure American energy security.

To illustrate the scope of this deregulation, consider the extraction of oil and natural gas in protected lands. Under Project 2025, regulations that restrict drilling in areas such as the Arctic National Wildlife Refuge could be relaxed or eliminated entirely, opening up vast tracts of previously protected wilderness to energy companies. The argument here is that by expanding drilling, the U.S. can reduce reliance on foreign oil and boost domestic energy production. However, the environmental impact is significant. Drilling in sensitive areas threatens local ecosystems, endangers wildlife, and risks contaminating water supplies. For residents near these extraction sites, this means an increase in pollution, potential health risks, and disruption of local economies that depend on tourism and recreation associated with protected lands.

Another example lies in the rollback of climate regulations aimed at curbing greenhouse gas emissions. Current regulations require power plants and other large industries to limit their carbon emissions, often through investments in cleaner technology or renewable energy. Under Project 2025, these regulations could be drastically reduced or removed, allowing industries to prioritize profit over environmental responsibility. The immediate effect would be a resurgence of high-emission industries, which could lead to increased air pollution, exacerbating respiratory issues and reducing air quality in affected communities. In a broader context, this approach would hinder U.S. participation in global climate initiatives, making it challenging for international efforts to achieve meaningful reductions in global warming.

Resource management policies are also on the chopping block under Project 2025. Protections for public lands and waterways, such as the Clean Water Act, could be weakened, making it easier for companies to discharge waste into rivers and lakes. This deregulation would impact water quality nationwide, especially in rural and economically disadvantaged communities that often lack the resources to mitigate environmental damage. For instance, the loosening of water quality regulations could lead to increased contamination from industrial runoffs, affecting drinking water supplies and agricultural irrigation.

In each of these examples, the environmental deregulation proposed by Project 2025 serves to prioritize immediate economic gains over the long-term health and sustainability of natural resources. While proponents may celebrate these changes as a win for business and economic freedom, the broader impacts include increased pollution, accelerated climate change, and the potential loss of irreplaceable natural habitats, not just for Americans but also for the global community that shares the planet.

The Dismantling of Consumer Protections and Labor Laws

Project 2025's deregulation agenda extends beyond environmental policy to encompass significant reductions in consumer protections and labor laws, two areas that affect nearly every American in their daily lives. At its core, this approach reflects a belief that consumers and businesses benefit most from a "buyer beware" model, where market forces rather than government regulations drive fairness and safety. However, the removal of these protections has serious implications for individuals who rely on government oversight to ensure that products, services, and working conditions meet minimum standards of safety and quality.

In terms of consumer protections, Project 2025's vision involves a dramatic reduction in the powers of agencies like the Consumer Financial Protection Bureau (CFPB), which was established to protect consumers from unfair, deceptive, or abusive practices, particularly in the financial sector. By limiting the CFPB's authority, Project 2025 would make it easier for banks and financial institutions to offer high-interest loans, deceptive credit products, and other services that could exploit vulnerable consumers. Take, for example, payday lending, an industry that often targets low-income communities with short-term, high-interest loans. Under reduced oversight, these businesses could charge higher interest rates and fees, trapping individuals in cycles of debt with little recourse.

Similarly, protections for food and drug safety, regulated by the FDA, could see substantial cuts. This means that companies producing food, pharmaceuticals, and personal care products may not be held to the same safety standards, increasing the risk of harmful products reaching consumers. A lack of stringent oversight could lead to more frequent product recalls, cases of contamination, and instances where unsafe products remain on the shelves longer, posing significant health risks to consumers.

Labor protections, another target of Project 2025's deregulation agenda, are critical in ensuring safe working conditions, fair wages, and protections against exploitation. Project 2025 aims to reduce the regulatory burden on businesses, which often translates to rolling back labor laws that govern workplace safety standards, minimum wage regulations, and overtime pay. For example, the Occupational Safety and Health Administration (OSHA), which enforces safety standards in workplaces, could see its power curtailed. In practice, this might mean fewer inspections, less enforcement of safety violations, and greater risk of injury for workers in industries like construction, manufacturing, and mining.

Minimum wage protections and overtime regulations could also be weakened. Project 2025 posits that reducing these requirements allows businesses to operate more freely and potentially hire more employees. However, in reality, this deregulation often results in lower wages and longer hours for workers, particularly in industries with low bargaining power like retail and hospitality. For a single mother working two jobs at a minimum wage, this could mean the difference between affording basic necessities or not, highlighting how deregulation disproportionately affects vulnerable populations.

These rollbacks in consumer protections and labor laws underscore Project 2025's philosophy of "individual responsibility" over collective safety. While proponents argue that deregulation fosters innovation and economic growth, critics point to the real-world consequences: increased financial vulnerability, unsafe products, and diminished worker rights.

How These Rollbacks Impact Everyday Americans and Global Environmental Efforts

The effects of these deregulation efforts reach deep into the lives of everyday Americans, influencing everything from the air they breathe to the products they buy and the conditions under which they work. By stripping away protections that have long been considered fundamental, Project 2025 puts the onus on individuals to navigate a landscape where corporate interests hold significant power and influence.

Imagine an American family in a small town reliant on local water sources for their drinking water. Under Project 2025's deregulation policies, a nearby manufacturing plant could discharge waste into rivers without stringent oversight, leading to contamination of the local water supply. Families may face increased health risks, from skin irritations to more severe conditions like cancer, as they are exposed to pollutants in their drinking water. For those with limited resources, finding safe alternatives becomes a struggle, highlighting the very real, human consequences of environmental deregulation.

On a global scale, the rollback of environmental protections in the U.S. undermines international climate commitments, making it more difficult for global initiatives to meet targets set by agreements like the Paris Climate Accord. The U.S., as one of the largest emitters of greenhouse gases, plays a pivotal role in global environmental efforts. A retreat from climate action under Project 2025 would mean increased greenhouse gas emissions, exacerbating the effects of climate change worldwide. Rising sea levels, intensified storms, and prolonged droughts would not only impact American communities but also those in vulnerable regions across the globe, from low-lying islands to drought-stricken areas in Africa and Asia.

Additionally, the reduction of consumer and labor protections creates an economy where individuals must fend for themselves against corporations with significantly more power. For example, without strong regulatory oversight, a worker in a factory could be exposed to unsafe machinery or harmful chemicals, increasing the risk of injury or illness. In a market without robust consumer protections, a senior citizen could unknowingly invest their life savings in a high-risk financial product, only to lose everything when the company fails to disclose the associated risks.

These changes create an America where individuals must shoulder the risks once managed by regulatory agencies. For those with means, the impact may be less visible; they can afford to mitigate risks through private alternatives, such as clean water systems or private legal representation. But for millions of Americans living paycheck to paycheck, these rollbacks mean a higher level of vulnerability and fewer safeguards against harm.

Project 2025's approach to rolling back regulatory protections may be framed as a drive for economic freedom and individual responsibility, but it introduces significant risks to public health, safety, and environmental sustainability. Through its deregulatory policies, Project 2025 envisions a government that prioritizes economic growth and corporate interests over protections for the environment, consumers, and workers. While proponents argue that these changes liberate businesses from burdensome regulations, the costs are borne by everyday Americans and the global community.

The impacts of these rollbacks are profound, touching nearly every aspect of life for Americansparticularly those who rely on the protections that government regulations provide. From environmental degradation and unsafe products to worker exploitation and financial insecurity, the risks of a deregulated America under Project 2025 are far-reaching. As we move forward, it is crucial to consider not only the short-term economic benefits but also the long-term consequences for society and the planet. In this context, Project 2025's deregulation agenda serves as a stark reminder of what is at stake in the ongoing debate over the role of government in safeguarding public interests.

CHAPTER FOUR

Judicial and Legislative Strategies for Long-Term Change

Project 2025's vision for America isn't just about immediate policy changes; it's about ensuring a conservative legacy that lasts well into the future. To achieve this, Project 2025 seeks to alter the fundamental structures of American governance through strategies that influence both the judiciary and the legislative process. These judicial and legislative maneuvers are designed to entrench conservative principles deeply within the American political system, creating an environment where opposition voices find it increasingly difficult to make themselves heard or to achieve meaningful change.

Expanding Influence in the Judiciary

One of the most enduring impacts of any administration is its influence on the judiciary. Unlike legislative or executive actions, judicial appointments are for life, meaning that judges installed in federal courts will continue to shape American law long after the appointing administration has left office. Project 2025 seeks to leverage this to its fullest by placing conservative judges in key judicial positions, thereby creating a legacy that could support conservative values for generations.

The Supreme Court is, of course, the crown jewel in this strategy. With lifetime appointments, the decisions made by the nine justices carry immense weight on issues such as abortion, LGBTQ+ rights, gun control, and environmental protections. By ensuring a conservative majority on the Court, Project 2025 can push forward decisions that align with conservative priorities, effectively making it more difficult for future administrations to reverse these policies. For example, the 2022 decision in *Dobbs v. Jackson Women's Health Organization*, which overturned *Roe v. Wade*, highlights the power of a conservative court. This ruling didn't just change a single policy; it reset the legal landscape surrounding reproductive rights, returning power to the states and creating a patchwork of access across the country. Project 2025 seeks more such rulings, ones that reshape not only specific policies but the very fabric of American jurisprudence.

But the strategy doesn't stop with the Supreme Court. Project 2025 also aims to fill the federal appeals courts and district courts with conservative judges who can influence decisions at all levels of the judiciary. The federal appeals courts are particularly critical because they serve as the last stop for most federal cases, as only a tiny fraction of cases make it to the Supreme Court. For instance, decisions on immigration policies, labor laws, and corporate regulations are often finalized at the appellate level, meaning that having a conservative majority in these courts ensures a broader implementation of conservative principles.

This strategy includes fostering partnerships with organizations like the Federalist Society, which has been instrumental in identifying and promoting conservative legal talent. By cultivating a network of conservative jurists, Project 2025 can ensure a steady stream of candidates who are ideologically aligned with its goals. Consider the appointments of Justices Brett Kavanaugh and Amy Coney Barrett, both of whom were highly recommended by conservative legal organizations and have since delivered rulings that reflect a conservative worldview. The careful selection and promotion of judges aligned with the ideology of Project 2025 ensure that conservative legal interpretations will influence American life for decades to come.

Legislative Maneuvers to Entrench Policies

Beyond the judiciary, Project 2025 aims to shape American governance through legislative maneuvers that fortify conservative power and restrict opposition. Gerrymandering, restrictive voter laws, and electoral reforms are central tools in this strategy, each one aimed at making it harder for opposition voices to break through or gain traction.

Gerrymandering as a Tool for Political Control

Gerrymandering, redrawing electoral district lines to favor a particular party, has long been used to consolidate power, but Project 2025 seeks to elevate it to a science. By drawing district boundaries in ways that cluster conservative voters together or dilute the impact of liberal voters, Project 2025 can create a structural advantage that lasts for years, even decades. For instance, in states like Texas and North Carolina, gerrymandered districts have led to a disproportionate number of conservative representatives compared to the actual voter demographics, effectively sidelining moderate and liberal voices.

Imagine a state where liberals and conservatives are split 50-50 among voters. In a fair system, representatives would reflect that split. However, through strategic gerrymandering, a state legislature can create districts where conservatives hold a majority in the vast majority of districts, turning a 50-50 voter split into an overwhelming conservative legislative majority. This manipulation of district lines makes it exceedingly difficult for opposition parties to gain representation, thereby entrenching conservative dominance regardless of shifts in public opinion.

Restrictive Voter Laws and Access Limitations

Project 2025 also seeks to implement voter laws that disproportionately affect certain demographics, particularly those more likely to vote for opposition candidates. This can include stricter voter ID laws, limits on early voting and mail-in voting, and purging voter rolls. The argument often centers around preventing voter fraud, but in reality, these laws make it harder for marginalized groups, such as low-income individuals, minorities, and young people, to participate in the democratic process.

Take the case of Wisconsin, where strict voter ID laws were shown to disproportionately impact African American and Latino voters, communities that historically lean Democratic. Similarly, the reduction of early voting hours or the closure of polling locations in urban areas, which tend to vote liberal, creates long lines and logistical challenges that discourage voter turnout. By implementing similar restrictions nationwide, Project 2025 seeks to tip the scales in favor of conservative voters, creating structural barriers that make it more difficult for the opposition to mobilize.

Electoral Reforms to Limit Opposition

In addition to gerrymandering and restrictive voter laws, Project 2025 advocates for electoral reforms that could cement conservative control at multiple levels of government. For example, there are proposals to change how electoral college votes are allocated, moving from a winner-takes-all system to a system where votes are distributed by congressional district. This change could advantage conservatives, particularly in swing states where rural, conservative districts could contribute more electoral votes than urban, liberal areas.

Another example is the push to limit the voting rights of individuals with past criminal convictions, a measure that disproportionately affects minority communities. Although some states have begun to restore voting rights to former felons, Project 2025 advocates argue for maintaining or even expanding these disenfranchisement laws as a means of "protecting electoral integrity." However, the effect is clear: by barring large segments of the population from voting, these laws suppress opposition voices and tilt elections toward conservative outcomes.

How These Strategies Shape Future Governance and Restrict Opposition

The cumulative effect of these judicial and legislative strategies is to create a political environment that is increasingly unassailable by opposition voices. By controlling the courts, Project 2025 ensures that challenges to conservative policies are less likely to succeed, as conservative judges interpret laws and the Constitution in ways that favor conservative values. This has profound implications for issues such as reproductive rights, LGBTQ+ protections, immigration, and environmental regulation, all of which may face significant setbacks in a judicial landscape that prioritizes conservative interpretations.

Meanwhile, through gerrymandering, restrictive voter laws, and electoral reforms, Project 2025 can make it harder for opposition candidates to win elections or enact policies that counter conservative interests. These legislative maneuvers are not just about winning the next election; they are about reshaping the political playing field in ways that keep opposition voices marginalized. When opposition voters are systematically prevented from achieving fair representation, the balance of power shifts decisively, creating a government that no longer reflects the diversity of American viewpoints but instead enshrines a narrow ideological perspective.

Consider the long-term effects of these strategies on American democracy. By limiting the channels through which opposition voices can gain power, either through legislative representation or through the courts, Project 2025 is effectively altering the nature of American governance. The resulting system is one in which power is centralized, dissent is minimized, and opposition voices are structurally disadvantaged, creating an environment where meaningful change becomes difficult, if not impossible, to achieve.

This shift toward an entrenched conservative power structure doesn't just impact current policy debates; it changes the fundamental fabric of American democracy. In a healthy democracy, power ebbs and flows between different ideologies and parties, each one reflecting the evolving views and values of the public. But under Project 2025's strategy, this natural dynamism is stifled. Instead, it creates a system where a single ideology can hold sway over multiple generations, regardless of changes in public opinion or shifts in societal values.

The judicial and legislative strategies outlined by Project 2025 represent a concerted effort to reshape American governance, making it harder for opposition voices to influence policy and law. Through the expansion of conservative influence in the judiciary, Project 2025 aims to create a legacy of legal rulings that reflect conservative values on critical issues. Meanwhile, through legislative maneuvers like gerrymandering, restrictive voter laws, and strategic electoral reforms, Project 2025 seeks to create a structural advantage that minimizes the impact of opposition voters and consolidates conservative power.

The implications of these strategies are profound. They don't just impact individual policies; they reshape the very mechanisms through which policy is made and contested. In doing so, Project 2025 aims to create a governance structure that is insulated from the checks and balances of a truly competitive political system. The result is a future where American governance may become less reflective of the people it serves, with a narrowing scope for dissenting voices to participate in meaningful ways.

For a democracy to thrive, it needs the ability to adapt, to reflect changing societal values, and to allow all voices to be heard. Project 2025's judicial and legislative strategies put this adaptability at risk. As Americans grapple with what this means for their future, understanding the depth and impact of these strategies is critical.

CHAPTER FIVE

The Role of Social Policy in Conservative Governance

In its quest to reshape America, Project 2025 goes beyond economic policies and regulatory changes, delving deeply into social policy. From immigration and education to healthcare and civil rights, social policies have always been fundamental battlegrounds in American politics. For Project 2025, they are seen as essential levers to mold the nation's cultural landscape according to conservative values. Let's explore how Project 2025's social policy objectives aim to shape immigration, education, and healthcare, restrict civil rights, and control cultural narratives to foster an environment in which conservative ideals prevail and alternative voices are minimized.

Policies on Immigration, Education, and Healthcare in Project 2025

Immigration: Tightening Borders and Limiting Pathways

Immigration has been a focal point in conservative policy, often cast as a matter of national security and cultural integrity. Under Project 2025, immigration policies seek to reduce both legal and illegal immigration, centralizing stricter regulations on entry, expanding border security, and limiting pathways to citizenship. The proposed framework pushes for increased funding and resources toward border enforcement and surveillance, mirroring the Trump-era priorities of physical barriers and enhanced patrols along the southern border. However, Project 2025 extends this by advocating for broader measures, including enhanced use of surveillance technology, expedited deportations, and even limiting family-based immigration channels, which historically have been the primary path for many immigrants.

For example, the reduction of asylum opportunities would have a profound impact on individuals fleeing violence or persecution, especially those from Latin America. By narrowing asylum qualifications and fast-tracking deportations, Project 2025 seeks to reduce the influx of immigrants, claiming it's necessary to protect American resources and job opportunities. However, this approach has significant social implications; it overlooks the contributions immigrants make in fields from agriculture to healthcare and adds barriers for individuals seeking safety and new opportunities in the U.S.

Education: A Push for Conservative Curricula and Policies

Education policy is another critical area where Project 2025 aims to make substantial changes. Its approach is focused on promoting "patriotic education," which emphasizes American exceptionalism, downplays historical injustices, and discourages teaching on topics like systemic racism or gender diversity. This education model aligns with efforts to curtail what proponents call "woke indoctrination" and what opponents recognize as legitimate discourse on historical and social issues.

Consider the debates around curricula related to history and social studies. In some states, educational guidelines now prohibit or limit discussions of slavery's impacts, the civil rights movement, and Indigenous history, claiming that such discussions sow division. Project 2025 expands on this trend, advocating for a standardized national curriculum that emphasizes conservative values, with a focus on patriotism, respect for authority, and traditional family structures. Supporters argue this approach fosters national pride and unity, while critics contend it whitewashes history, limits critical thinking, and leaves students unprepared to understand and address contemporary social issues.

Further, Project 2025 promotes school choice initiatives, such as voucher programs that channel public funding into private and religious schools, many of which align with conservative values. This redirection of funds could deplete resources for public schools, particularly in low-income communities, limiting educational opportunities for vulnerable students. While school choice supporters argue this gives families more options, detractors point out that it often leads to a stratified education system where public institutions are underfunded, perpetuating inequity and limiting social mobility.

Healthcare: Defunding Public Programs and Promoting Privatization

In healthcare, Project 2025 seeks to minimize government intervention by scaling back programs such as Medicaid and the Affordable Care Act (ACA), pushing instead for market-driven solutions. The aim is to create a more "efficient" system that encourages personal responsibility and free-market competition. This approach involves reducing federal oversight, cutting subsidies, and rolling back mandates that require insurers to cover essential health benefits.

For instance, under Project 2025, mental health coverage and maternity care, often required under ACA, could become optional, leaving individuals to pay more out of pocket for these services. Proponents argue that reducing government intervention will decrease overall costs by fostering competition, but opponents warn that without federal standards, vulnerable populations may lose access to necessary care. Such changes may especially impact low-income families who rely on these services for access to affordable healthcare, including preventive services that help maintain public health and reduce long-term healthcare costs.

Restrictions on Civil Rights

LGBTQ+ Rights: Rolling Back Protections

Project 2025 takes a strong stance on LGBTQ+ issues, with plans to reverse protections established in recent years. This includes reducing anti-discrimination protections in workplaces, schools, and healthcare settings, which have enabled LGBTQ+ individuals to access services without fear of bias or mistreatment. The approach aligns with conservative beliefs around traditional family values and seeks to limit the recognition of diverse gender identities and sexual orientations within federal policies.

For example, Project 2025 supports rescinding protections for transgender individuals that allow them to access healthcare or use facilities that align with their gender identity. This rollback could affect everything from access to gender-affirming healthcare to participation in sports or use of public restrooms. Supporters view this as a way to preserve traditional family values, while opponents argue it marginalizes an already vulnerable population and undermines individual freedoms.

Reproductive Rights: Limiting Access to Abortion and Contraception

On reproductive rights, Project 2025 aims to build on recent Supreme Court decisions, like *Dobbs v. Jackson Women's Health Organization*, which overturned *Roe v. Wade* and left abortion rights up to individual states. Project 2025 advocates for a national approach to limiting abortion, encouraging legislation that would restrict it in as many states as possible and advocating for more rigorous limits on federal funding for contraceptive services through programs like Title X.

For example, this could mean fewer federally funded health clinics that offer birth control and counseling on reproductive health, disproportionately affecting low-income individuals and those in rural areas. By limiting these services, Project 2025 restricts reproductive choices, aligning with its conservative values. However, critics argue that these policies don't consider the full scope of women's healthcare needs, potentially leading to adverse health outcomes and limiting personal autonomy.

Religious Freedom: Broadening Conscientious Objections

Project 2025 places a strong emphasis on religious freedom, advocating for policies that allow individuals and businesses to deny services based on their religious beliefs. This policy shift, known as expanding "conscientious objections," enables healthcare providers, employers, and businesses to refuse services that conflict with their religious views. While advocates argue this protects religious rights, opponents warn it could lead to widespread discrimination, especially against LGBTQ+ individuals and women seeking reproductive care.

For instance, under these policies, a healthcare provider might refuse to provide contraception, or a business owner could decline service to a same-sex couple. The extension of religious exemptions could result in a society where discrimination is legalized under the guise of religious freedom, effectively allowing personal beliefs to override individual rights and limiting access to services for marginalized groups.

The Cultural War

At the heart of Project 2025's social policy approach is the desire to shape and control cultural narratives, often referred to as the "culture war." This strategy involves influencing media, education, and public discourse to establish a dominant conservative perspective that defines what it means to be American. From promoting "patriotic education" to regulating content on social media, Project 2025 uses various tools to frame public opinion and minimize dissent.

Media and Social Media: Amplifying Conservative Voices

Project 2025 advocates for a strong presence in both traditional media and digital spaces to amplify conservative viewpoints. Through alliances with conservative media outlets and calls for reduced content moderation on social media, Project 2025 seeks to ensure that conservative messages reach broader audiences while countering what it perceives as "liberal bias" in mainstream media. The emphasis on "free speech" policies on social media platforms, for example, is seen as a way to protect conservative views, but it may also allow the spread of misinformation or hate speech under the banner of free expression.

Consider recent attempts by conservative groups to pressure social media companies to reduce content moderation, claiming that restrictions disproportionately target conservative voices. This approach creates a polarized media landscape where narratives diverge sharply, making it more challenging for the public to access balanced information. By controlling narratives, Project 2025 aims to shape public perceptions in ways that align with its broader goals.

The Rise of "Patriotic Education" and Historical Revisionism

Project 2025 also targets the educational system, pushing for curricula that celebrate American exceptionalism and downplay or ignore the more complex, sometimes dark aspects of U.S. history, such as slavery, Indigenous displacement, and systemic racism. By influencing how history is taught, Project 2025 aims to instill a specific worldview in young Americans, one that promotes loyalty, patriotism, and a respect for traditional values over critical thinking and open discourse.

This approach is exemplified by the "1776 Commission," which sought to promote a patriotic view of history as an alternative to the more critical narratives found in projects like The New York Times' 1619 Project. Project 2025 sees this kind of "patriotic education" as essential to fostering a unified national identity, but critics argue it limits students' understanding of the full American story, leaving them ill-prepared to engage with complex social issues.

Project 2025's approach to social policy seeks to create a cultural landscape in which conservative values are both normalized and legally entrenched. By reshaping immigration, education, and healthcare policies, and by rolling back protections for civil rights,

Project 2025 aims to mold an American society where traditional values prevail and alternative viewpoints are minimized. This strategy not only impacts the policies themselves but also influences the cultural narratives that define America's collective identity.

At stake is more than just policy; it's the direction of the nation's moral and cultural compass. Whether America remains a pluralistic society or trends toward a more monolithic, conservative vision depends on how these policies are implemented and whether they are embraced or resisted by the public.

CHAPTER SIX

Strengthening Domestic Surveillance and Policing

As Project 2025 seeks to consolidate power and secure its vision for America, one of the cornerstones of its strategy is the expansion of domestic surveillance and law enforcement powers. The driving belief behind this push is that greater control over the population is necessary to maintain national security, protect public order, and preserve conservative values. But this focus on increased surveillance and police power raises significant concerns about individual freedoms, the erosion of privacy rights, and the potential for unchecked governmental authority to quash dissent and enforce compliance.

Expanding Domestic Surveillance and Law Enforcement Powers

The Rise of a Surveillance State

In the name of national security, Project 2025 proposes sweeping changes to how the government monitors its citizens. This shift toward a surveillance state seeks to provide authorities with the tools to track, monitor, and potentially suppress any activity deemed subversive or harmful to the regime. The idea is that the government can prevent threats before they manifest by expanding its ability to observe private individuals and groups, both online and in the real world.

This policy, though framed as a defense against domestic terrorism and violent extremism, introduces new and worrying possibilities for overreach. Surveillance programs under Project 2025 could increase the use of technology such as facial recognition, predictive policing, and data mining to identify and track individuals. For example, just as the post-9/11 world saw an expansion of the Patriot Act to facilitate surveillance of individuals suspected of terrorism, Project 2025 would expand these powers to include tracking citizens who are perceived to be "anti-government" or hold progressive views.

Take the example of mass surveillance on social media platforms. In recent years, the U.S. government has taken steps to partner with tech companies to monitor online behavior under the guise of counterterrorism and public safety. Under Project 2025, these practices could be ramped up significantly, allowing government agencies to gather and analyze vast amounts of personal data, ranging from your browsing history to your social media activity, without a warrant or probable cause.

The extension of these surveillance tools could extend to monitoring phone conversations, emails, and even the movements of private citizens through their digital devices. The logic is that preventing violent threats and protecting national security requires a near-complete picture of individuals' behavior, but in practice, this would create a chilling atmosphere of constant monitoring, where personal privacy becomes a relic of the past.

Expanded Law Enforcement Powers and Their Reach

Project 2025 envisions law enforcement with increased authority to investigate, detain, and disrupt any perceived threats to the new regime. This includes expanding the role of federal agencies like the FBI, Department of Homeland Security (DHS), and Immigration and Customs Enforcement (ICE) in matters traditionally handled at the local level. The idea is to streamline the enforcement of conservative policies and make sure that national security concerns trump local jurisdictions or individual rights.

For example, the federal government might provide local police with more military-grade technology, such as surveillance drones and armored vehicles, or grant them greater leeway to act without oversight in pursuit of "threats." Under Project 2025, local law enforcement would be empowered not just to respond to crime but to actively intervene in social movements, protests, or even political dissent that challenge the administration.

Take the example of the Black Lives Matter protests that gained national attention in 2020. Under Project 2025, federal agencies could take a more prominent role in quelling such protests, using surveillance tools and coordinating with local police to infiltrate and monitor protest groups before they even gather in public spaces. This type of preemptive action could lead to more aggressive tactics against dissenting groups, criminalizing legitimate protests under the guise of national security.

Implications for Privacy Rights, Freedom of Speech, and Activism

The Erosion of Privacy Rights

At the heart of Project 2025's surveillance strategy is a systematic erosion of privacy rights. Americans have long prized their right to privacy, viewing it as a safeguard against government overreach. However, under Project 2025, this right could be curtailed in the name of security and public safety.

Consider how the U.S. government has already collected data on individuals through surveillance programs like PRISM, which was revealed in 2013. Project 2025 would expand such programs, creating a more extensive network of data collection, all without due process. For example, the government might justify tapping into private communications, like emails, phone calls, and even financial records, arguing that such measures are necessary to ensure public safety in an increasingly digital world.

The potential for abuse of this data is enormous. Without adequate oversight or safeguards, the government could misuse information to silence opposition, monitor activists, and target individuals based on their political or social beliefs. This could mean that individuals critical of the administration, whether journalists, activists, or even ordinary citizens, could find themselves under surveillance simply for expressing dissenting opinions.

Restricting Freedom of Speech and Press

The expansion of surveillance also has profound implications for freedom of speech and the press. As government surveillance increases, people may feel less comfortable expressing themselves freely, knowing that their communications, movements, and even online activity are being monitored. This chilling effect can discourage individuals from participating in public discourse, particularly on sensitive topics like politics, human rights, or social justice issues.

This can be especially harmful to journalists and whistleblowers. A free press is essential to holding the government accountable, but under Project 2025, reporters could face heightened risks of surveillance or intimidation for reporting on issues critical of the administration. As seen with the use of the Espionage Act against whistleblowers like Edward Snowden, the U.S. government has historically targeted individuals for exposing uncomfortable truths. Project 2025 could escalate this tendency, putting press freedoms and the right to free expression under serious threat.

For example, imagine a journalist reporting on government misconduct who learns that their private communications with sources have been monitored by government agencies. The fear of surveillance could lead to self-censorship or an inability to protect sensitive sources. In such an environment, independent journalism would be stifled, and the public would be deprived of critical information about how the government operates.

Impact on Activism and Social Movements

Social movements play an important role in challenging the status quo and advocating for progressive change. Historically, groups like the Civil Rights Movement, feminist movements, and labor unions have relied on free speech, organizing, and protest to advance their causes. However, under Project 2025, such movements could face heightened scrutiny, surveillance, and repression.

For example, environmental activists, labor organizers, or racial justice groups that frequently challenge powerful institutions might find themselves targeted by law enforcement agencies. Surveillance tools could be used to monitor meetings, infiltrate social movements, and disrupt peaceful demonstrations before they even take place. Under Project 2025, such groups may find themselves under the constant threat of legal action, having their communications intercepted, or being investigated for "subversive" activities.

This creates a dangerous precedent where activism is criminalized simply because it challenges the prevailing political narrative. Instead of fostering an open, democratic society where diverse views are welcomed, Project 2025 seeks to control public dissent through surveillance and police power, thereby stifling the very activism that has been crucial in advancing civil rights and social progress.

Militarization of Policing and Its Role in Enforcing Project 2025 Policies

The Use of Military-Grade Equipment in Civilian Policing

One of the most contentious aspects of Project 2025's approach to law enforcement is the proposal to further militarize local police forces. By providing state and local law enforcement agencies with military-grade equipment like armored vehicles, assault rifles, and drones, the project seeks to enhance their capacity to control and suppress any perceived threat to the administration.

For example, during the 2020 protests following George Floyd's death, the use of military-grade gear by police forces led to a violent crackdown on demonstrators, which many viewed as an overreaction. Under Project 2025, this trend would not only continue but be institutionalized. The justification for this militarization is often framed as protecting law enforcement from violent criminals or domestic terrorists. However, the reality is that these weapons of war could be used against everyday citizens simply expressing their constitutional right to protest.

The use of military-style tactics in civilian policing could erode trust in law enforcement, especially in marginalized communities who are disproportionately affected by police violence. As seen with the controversy surrounding the Department of Homeland Security's deployment of federal agents to Portland in 2020, militarized policing often leads to unnecessary violence and further divides communities from law enforcement.

Policing as a Tool for Political Control

Project 2025 envisions a more politically aligned law enforcement apparatus, one that can act as a force for enforcing its policies and stifling opposition. This creates a dangerous precedent where law enforcement is no longer seen as a neutral arbiter of justice but as a political tool used to suppress any resistance to the agenda of those in power. This scenario mirrors authoritarian regimes around the world, where police and military forces serve as the backbone of political control.

For example, under the Trump administration, the use of federal agents in cities like Portland and Washington D.C. was framed as necessary to restore order, but it was widely viewed as an attempt to silence dissent and intimidate critics. Project 2025 could escalate this trend, using law enforcement to crack down on opposition movements and civil rights groups under the guise of maintaining national security.

The expansion of domestic surveillance and policing is one of the most significant and troubling aspects of Project 2025. While framed as necessary for national security and public order, these measures come with deep costs to privacy, civil rights, and the health of American democracy. The more surveillance and policing are centralized under the executive branch, the greater the risk becomes that the government will use its power not just to maintain law and order but to consolidate political control and eliminate dissent.

As we move forward in this exploration of Project 2025, it's critical to consider the long-term consequences of these policies. Surveillance and militarized policing are not just tools for enforcing the law, they are instruments of power, capable of reshaping American society into one that values obedience over freedom, surveillance over privacy, and control over dissent. The implications for individual rights, democracy, and social movements are profound, and they are issues that Americans must grapple with as they consider the future of their nation.

CHAPTER SEVEN

Foreign Policy Reorientation: Nationalism and Isolationism

In the blueprint of Project 2025, America's foreign policy is being reimagined through the lens of nationalism and isolationism. As the United States grapples with internal political polarization and growing challenges to its global influence, the architects of Project 2025 see a shift away from traditional multilateralism and international cooperation in favor of an America-first approach. Let's explore how the reorientation of U.S. foreign policy under Project 2025 seeks to reshape America's relationships with its allies, redefine its stance on trade and defense, and adopt a more insular approach to global issues, paving the way for an isolationist and nationalistic America.

How Project 2025 Envisions American Engagement with Global Allies and Adversaries

Under Project 2025, the U.S. foreign policy would move away from diplomatic engagement in international institutions, such as the United Nations or the World Trade Organization, toward a more transactional, interests-based model. The idea is to prioritize

American interests above all, even if that means undermining long-standing alliances or withdrawing from multilateral agreements.

For example, the Heritage Foundation and Project 2025 supporters argue that America has often sacrificed its sovereignty to international organizations, compromising its national identity and economic strength. Under this framework, U.S. foreign policy would increasingly favor bilateral agreements over multinational collaborations. This would mean a withdrawal from many global commitments, including trade deals and international environmental accords that do not serve immediate American interests.

The notion of "America First" echoes President Trump's own foreign policy stance during his presidency, where he withdrew the U.S. from the Paris Climate Agreement and renegotiated the North American Free Trade Agreement (NAFTA) into the United States-Mexico-Canada Agreement (USMCA). This policy approach would only intensify under Project 2025, as the country steps back from its traditional leadership role on the global stage.

On the global adversary front, Project 2025 proposes a more aggressive posture toward countries like China and Russia, viewing these nations as strategic competitors. However, the approach would be more confrontational, characterized by a belief that the U.S. must act unilaterally to safeguard its position, rather than work through alliances. For example, the project may call for a harder stance on trade imbalances with China or stronger military deterrents against Russian expansionism, but with less regard for coalition-building or diplomatic negotiation. The focus would shift to power projection rather than cooperative engagement, intensifying the ideological divide between democratic and authoritarian regimes.

Shifts in Trade, Defense, and Immigration Policy under a Nationalist Agenda

Trade Policy: Protectionism and Economic Sovereignty

At the heart of Project 2025's economic nationalism lies the desire to shield the American economy from what its supporters see as the negative impacts of globalization. Trade policy would be rewritten to prioritize American jobs and industries over free-market principles or global cooperation. This means the country would pursue protectionist measures, such as tariffs, quotas, and import restrictions, to ensure that foreign competition doesn't undermine domestic industries.

Take, for instance, the trade war with China during the Trump administration, which saw the imposition of tariffs on billions of dollars in Chinese imports. This protectionist policy was aimed at reducing the trade deficit and pushing China to reform its trade practices. Project 2025 would likely expand on these policies by not only targeting adversaries like China but also renegotiating trade deals with traditional allies to ensure they align with America's economic priorities.

For example, the U.S. could impose tariffs on European Union (EU) imports if European nations are seen as undercutting American industries. The goal would be to stimulate American manufacturing and reduce reliance on foreign goods, particularly in industries like steel, technology, and pharmaceuticals.

This protectionist trade policy would also affect the global supply chain. By prioritizing domestic production over imported goods, Project 2025 envisions a reshaping of manufacturing practices, with industries like technology, automobiles, and agriculture increasingly shifting from global markets to a more self-sustaining, national framework.

Defense Policy: A Shift Toward Unilateral Power Projection

Project 2025's vision for defense policy is also shaped by a nationalist approach, focused on strengthening U.S. military capabilities while reducing reliance on international coalitions like NATO. The goal is to reassert U.S. military dominance, but with a more isolationist mindset, emphasizing American strength without the encumbrance of shared responsibility or multilateral commitments.

One of the proposals within Project 2025 would be to significantly reduce the U.S.'s military footprint in places like Europe and the Middle East. The idea here is that these regions no longer pose the same strategic threats to U.S. interests, and the American taxpayer should not bear the financial burden of defending other countries. Instead, military resources would be reallocated to counter perceived threats closer to home, such as a more assertive China in the South China Sea or a resurgent Russia.

This "America First" defense policy would also involve ramping up the modernization of the U.S. military, with an emphasis on cyber warfare capabilities, missile defense systems, and space technology. The idea is that America must remain the global superpower in defense, but it must do so on its own terms, without the political and economic entanglements of NATO or other alliances.

Immigration Policy: Tightening Borders and Prioritizing American Workers

Under Project 2025, immigration policy would be more closely aligned with nationalistic principles, with a strong focus on limiting immigration to protect American workers and reduce the perceived strain on public services. This would include stricter border enforcement, restrictions on visa programs, and a reduction in the number of refugees and asylum seekers allowed into the country.

The focus would be on ensuring that immigration benefits the U.S. economy by prioritizing skilled workers, particularly in industries like technology, healthcare, and engineering. Conversely, immigration from countries seen as "high-risk" or less economically advantageous to the U.S. would be sharply reduced. For instance, the project might argue for ending the Diversity Visa Program, which currently provides visas to people from countries with historically low rates of immigration to the U.S.

In addition, Project 2025 would likely push for significant reforms to the asylum process, with proposals to end or significantly limit sanctuary cities, expedite deportations, and crack down on illegal immigration. These policies would reflect a shift from seeing immigration as a human rights issue to framing it as a security and economic issue, with a clear preference for immigrants who contribute directly to the American economy.

The Potential Global Impact of a More Isolationist U.S.

Project 2025's isolationist vision for America's foreign policy holds profound implications for global geopolitics. The retreat of the U.S. from its leadership role would likely lead to a realignment of global power structures. Without America's active participation in international organizations and agreements, countries and regions that rely on U.S. influence may seek out new alliances, potentially with authoritarian powers like China or Russia.

For example, if the U.S. were to disengage from NATO, European countries might seek alternative security arrangements or increase their defense spending to maintain their own military capabilities. In Asia, countries like Japan and South Korea could be left vulnerable to Chinese or North Korean aggression without a strong U.S. military presence in the region. This could also open the door for China to expand its Belt and Road Initiative (BRI) and extend its influence over global trade routes, especially in the developing world.

On the economic front, a U.S. that embraces protectionism could set off a wave of retaliatory tariffs and trade wars, potentially undermining the global economy. By pulling back from multilateral trade agreements, the U.S. would isolate itself from its largest trading partners and create friction in global supply chains. This could lead to inflationary pressures, higher costs for consumers, and a slowdown in economic growth worldwide.

Moreover, Project 2025's withdrawal from international climate agreements like the Paris Accord would likely undermine global efforts to address climate change. As one of the world's largest emitters of greenhouse gases, U.S. actions, or inactions, on climate policy play a crucial role in global environmental sustainability. If the U.S. steps back from its leadership role, countries may feel less pressure to meet their own commitments to reduce emissions, further accelerating global warming and environmental degradation.

Project 2025's foreign policy shift toward nationalism and isolationism represents a seismic shift in America's approach to global leadership. By prioritizing American interests and withdrawing from international cooperation, the U.S. risks alienating its allies, weakening global institutions, and undermining efforts to address pressing global challenges like climate change and security threats.

While proponents of Project 2025 argue that this approach will strengthen the U.S. by focusing on national sovereignty and economic independence, the long-term consequences could be destabilizing not only for America but for the world. As we move into an era defined by shifting power dynamics and emerging global challenges, the success or failure of Project 2025's foreign policy will have lasting implications for America's place in the world, and the global order as a whole.

CHAPTER EIGHT

Mobilizing the Conservative Base

The success of Project 2025 hinges not only on the policies and institutional changes it seeks to implement but also on its ability to effectively rally support and manage opposition. To solidify the conservative base and achieve long-lasting influence, the project relies on a multifaceted strategy of mobilization, media control, and targeted suppression of dissent. Let's examine the key strategies for building loyalty among the conservative base, the powerful role of media partnerships and social media in shaping public opinion, and the tactics Project 2025 might employ to counter and silence opposition.

Strategies for Rallying Support and Suppressing Opposition

Project 2025 recognizes that building and maintaining a committed base of supporters is crucial. This is particularly true for political movements that seek to implement sweeping changes across various branches of government. Project 2025 employs several strategies to foster loyalty among conservative voters and effectively counter opposition, painting dissenters as threats to the American way of life. This tactic has two core aims: to deepen the commitment of the conservative base and to portray opposition as un-American.

Rallying the Conservative Base

At the heart of this approach is the narrative that Project 2025 is a movement to "restore American greatness." This is reminiscent of former President Trump's "Make America Great Again" slogan, which successfully rallied millions of Americans by tapping into concerns about cultural change, economic dislocation, and fears of losing national identity. Project 2025 takes this concept further, aiming to create an emotional connection with its supporters by emphasizing conservative values like patriotism, religious faith, and individual freedom. For example, rallies, town halls, and grassroots events are used not only to spread policy details but also to evoke a sense of nostalgia for a perceived better past and a fear of a chaotic future if the "right" values aren't upheld.

Additionally, the architects of Project 2025 often frame policy issues in terms of personal, moral imperatives. Take immigration reform, for example. By casting immigration policy as a defense of "law and order" and national identity, Project 2025 taps into deeply rooted fears and values. Similarly, by framing its deregulatory goals as a fight for "economic freedom" and a pushback against "big government," Project 2025 creates an environment where the base feels that supporting these policies is a moral obligation, not just a political choice.

Suppressing Opposition

Suppressing dissent is equally important to Project 2025's success, as it faces criticism from various factions within and outside the U.S. By framing opposition as radical or dangerous, Project 2025 can discourage critical voices and isolate its detractors. One tactic used to stifle opposition is labeling critics as "enemies of the people," a phrase that has historically been effective in authoritarian regimes as well as in certain conservative circles in the United States.

For instance, individuals or groups advocating for expanded civil rights, environmental protections, or immigration reform might be labeled as part of the "radical left" or as undermining traditional American values. Such language can discourage moderate conservatives and undecided voters from supporting these causes, fostering a hostile environment for activists and critics. Project 2025 also uses targeted legislation to make public dissent more difficult; for example, passing laws that increase penalties for protest-related activities or that classify certain demonstrations as "domestic terrorism" are among the tactics it could deploy to curb vocal opposition and public protests.

Media Partnerships, Grassroots Organizations, and the Role of Social Media

Media Partnerships and Narrative Control

Media is a powerful tool in Project 2025's strategy to shape public opinion and maintain control over the narrative. Conservative media outlets play a key role in delivering messages that resonate with the base while minimizing coverage of opposition voices. Project 2025's success rests on partnerships with conservative-leaning media outlets that amplify its policies, defend its actions, and discredit critics.

The project collaborates with established news networks, like Fox News, and newer digital media platforms that appeal to younger conservatives, like Newsmax and The Daily Wire. These partnerships ensure that Project 2025's narrative reaches a wide audience, blending news coverage with opinion pieces that reinforce the project's worldview. For instance, stories might highlight the success of deregulation in "freeing" small businesses from bureaucratic red tape while ignoring the potential downsides for environmental or consumer protections. This controlled coverage makes it difficult for alternative perspectives to reach conservative audiences.

Project 2025 also cultivates relationships with conservative radio hosts, bloggers, and influencers, using them to amplify key messages. This strategy leverages the influence of figures like Ben Shapiro or Candace Owens, who have significant followings on YouTube, Twitter, and Instagram. By promoting Project 2025's policies and framing opposition voices as untrustworthy or radical, these influencers help to sustain and spread the project's ideals.

The Role of Grassroots Organizations

Grassroots organizations are another cornerstone of Project 2025's mobilization strategy. These organizations connect with local communities across the country, building a solid foundation of support at the neighborhood level. Organizations like Turning Point USA, Moms for Liberty, and conservative church groups are instrumental in promoting Project 2025's goals on issues ranging from school curricula to voting laws. These groups hold events, organize protests, and lead social media campaigns that rally community members around Project 2025's key themes, such as religious liberty, parental rights, and traditional family values.

Grassroots organizations also help Project 2025 sidestep criticism of being a top-down, elitist movement. By engaging local leaders and community influencers, Project 2025 creates the appearance of a bottom-up, populist movement, even though many of its ideas are crafted within well-funded think tanks like the Heritage Foundation.

Social Media: A Modern Platform for Control and Mobilization

Social media serves as the virtual battlefield for Project 2025's mobilization and narrative control. Through platforms like Twitter (X), Facebook, and Instagram, the project reaches millions instantly, tailoring its message to specific demographics. For younger audiences, Project 2025's messages might be infused with themes of "freedom" and "patriotism" in engaging formats, like memes and short videos. For older audiences, the focus might shift to safeguarding traditional values and fighting government overreach.

Project 2025 uses social media not only to promote its policies but also to attack its critics. This can include campaigns that flood comment sections of opposing viewpoints with counterarguments or trolling tactics that delegitimize dissenting opinions. In some cases, these tactics might go further, orchestrating online harassment campaigns against journalists, activists, or politicians who speak out against Project 2025. By controlling the narrative on social media, Project 2025 creates an environment where its supporters feel engaged and validated, while its opponents may feel marginalized and discouraged from speaking out.

Countering Public Dissent and Activism Through Rhetoric and Policy

Project 2025 takes a dual approach to suppressing dissent, combining rhetoric that delegitimizes critics with targeted policies that restrict activism. By painting opponents as a threat to the stability and values of the nation, Project 2025 sets the stage for policies aimed at limiting protest and activism.

Rhetoric: The Power of Framing and Language

Rhetoric is one of Project 2025's primary tools for discouraging public dissent. By framing opponents as "unpatriotic" or labeling their causes as "radical," Project 2025 attempts to stigmatize activism and drive a wedge between the conservative base and any ideas that diverge from the project's agenda. Language that characterizes environmental activists as "extremists," for instance, can be used to justify policies that limit or penalize protest activities related to environmental causes.

Moreover, by co-opting the language of freedom and patriotism, Project 2025 can reshape public discourse around who is entitled to those ideals. Critics of the project are often painted as attempting to undermine "traditional" American values, while supporters are positioned as the defenders of those values. This kind of language makes it difficult for opposing voices to find common ground, as they are cast not as Americans with differing views, but as threats to the nation's moral and cultural fabric.

Policy: Suppressing Dissent through Legislative Actions

In addition to rhetorical strategies, Project 2025 promotes policies aimed at making public dissent and activism increasingly difficult. One method is through laws that impose heavy penalties on protests deemed disruptive or dangerous. For instance, under Project 2025, states might see an increase in anti-protest laws that criminalize "unlawful assembly" or even reclassify certain acts of protest as domestic terrorism.

For example, Project 2025 could support "anti-riot" legislation that penalizes individuals participating in large-scale protests with jail time and hefty fines. Even peaceful demonstrations could face restrictions under the guise of public safety. Such policies effectively deter individuals from protesting out of fear of legal repercussions. This tactic is particularly effective in silencing grassroots activism and opposition groups that rely on protest as a primary method of expression.

Another policy approach involves cutting off funding sources for organizations that support causes contrary to Project 2025's goals. This tactic could target nonprofits, advocacy groups, and other civil society organizations by introducing tax regulations or other bureaucratic hurdles that make it difficult for them to operate. For instance, increased IRS scrutiny of organizations deemed "politically radical" or legislative action that limits public funding for activist groups could force them to scale back their operations or close altogether.

Project 2025's mobilization efforts represent a sophisticated blend of narrative control, grassroots engagement, and suppression of dissent. Through its media partnerships, rhetoric, and policy strategies, Project 2025 aims to cultivate a committed, loyal base while creating an environment hostile to opposition voices. This approach not only reinforces its hold on power but also fosters a culture where the conservative base sees itself as defenders of a moral and nationalistic vision for America.

The consequences of these mobilization tactics are far-reaching. By amplifying conservative ideals and framing opposition as a threat, Project 2025 reshapes the social and political landscape in a way that narrows public discourse. Critics of the movement find themselves increasingly marginalized, while supporters are galvanized, believing they are part of a righteous cause to "save"

America. In this environment, true dialogue and democratic debate are at risk, as the political arena becomes a battleground defined by strict ideological lines, where Project 2025 supporters and opponents are pitted against each other as never before.

CHAPTER NINE

Lessons from Authoritarian Regimes

As Project 2025 sets out a roadmap to consolidate control over American institutions, the strategies it promotes echo tactics used by authoritarian regimes throughout history. By examining examples from authoritarian movements across the globe and across time, we can draw a clear line from past regimes to the present-day ambitions of Project 2025. Let's explore these parallels and considers how Project 2025 applies these strategies to reshape American governance, while also projecting what the future might look like if these ideas fully take root.

Comparative Analysis: Echoes of Authoritarian Playbooks from History

Authoritarian regimes have historically shared certain strategies to consolidate power and maintain control, such as centralizing authority, controlling narratives, restricting opposition, and using legal frameworks to suppress dissent. Several prominent examples illustrate how these tactics have played out in other countries and reveal similarities with Project 2025's proposed policies.

Centralization of Power

One of the first steps taken by many authoritarian regimes is the centralization of authority within a single branch of government. In the 1930s, for instance, Adolf Hitler and his allies dismantled checks on executive power, weakening the German parliament and judiciary to create a government with a singular, unquestioned leader. Similarly, Vladimir Putin's government in Russia moved rapidly to centralize power in the presidency, stripping authority from regional governments and installing loyalists in critical positions across the state. In both cases, centralization allowed these leaders to enact their agendas without significant opposition or interference from other branches of government.

Project 2025 mirrors these centralization tactics by proposing structural changes to the executive branch that increase presidential control over federal agencies and the civil service. Policies like the "Schedule F" initiative give the president the power to dismiss federal employees who are deemed "disloyal" or "obstructive." Such changes could turn federal agencies into tools of executive will, much like state organs in historical authoritarian regimes, where leadership loyalty becomes more important than qualifications or adherence to nonpartisan principles.

Controlling Media and Information

Controlling public perception is a hallmark of authoritarian regimes. In China, the government tightly controls all forms of media, censoring critical perspectives while promoting narratives that bolster the Chinese Communist Party. Similarly, in the 1920s and '30s, Italy's Mussolini used state media to promote fascist ideology and drown out dissent. These regimes show how controlling information flow enables the ruling party or leader to set the national agenda and shield itself from criticism.

Project 2025 adopts similar methods, emphasizing alliances with sympathetic media outlets to create a consistent, supportive narrative around its policies. By building close ties with conservative news organizations and social media influencers, Project 2025 seeks to flood the media landscape with content that reinforces its values while discrediting opposing views. This approach echoes the propaganda machines of past authoritarian regimes, where positive stories are pushed, and criticism is minimized or framed as a "threat" to national stability.

Restricting Opposition and Political Dissent

In authoritarian settings, suppressing opposition parties and activists is critical to ensuring that the ruling government faces minimal challenge. In Turkey, President Recep Tayyip Erdoğan's government has imprisoned opposition leaders, shuttered independent media outlets, and even extended these restrictions into the judiciary to prevent judicial challenges to his policies. This gradual elimination of dissenting voices enables authoritarian leaders to reshape the country without pushback.

In the United States, Project 2025's architects have similarly proposed policies that would restrict opposition through legal and social means. By passing restrictive voting laws, expanding surveillance on activist groups, and bolstering penalties for protest, Project 2025 draws from the same authoritarian playbook. It frames these measures as necessary for "public safety" and "election integrity," echoing the justifications used by Erdoğan and others who have limited civil liberties to maintain control.

Use of Legal Frameworks to Legitimize Power

Authoritarian regimes often create legal structures to provide a veneer of legitimacy to their actions. In Hungary, Viktor Orbán has rewritten the country's constitution multiple times, reshaping laws to entrench his party's control. These changes allow Orbán to maintain power while claiming legitimacy, as his actions technically fall within Hungary's legal framework, even if they subvert democratic principles.

Project 2025 adopts a similar approach, using the U.S. legal system to entrench conservative power. Its proponents advocate for judicial appointments and legislative maneuvers to ensure that conservative policies are legally unassailable. By reshaping the judiciary and leveraging legislative tools like gerrymandering, Project 2025 can construct a system where its control appears legal, even as it undermines democratic norms.

How Project 2025 Draws Upon These Principles for Consolidating Control

Project 2025 doesn't operate in a vacuum. Its architects are well aware of how authoritarian strategies have played out historically, and they draw upon these methods to create a model tailored for the United States. By studying authoritarian regimes, Project 2025 has identified and adapted these principles to build a long-lasting conservative government in a democratic society.

Consolidating Control Over Federal Agencies

Project 2025 seeks to remake federal agencies in the image of the executive, following the model of authoritarian regimes that replaced civil servants with loyalists. The "Schedule F" initiative, for example, allows Project 2025 to create a workforce that is loyal to the sitting administration rather than the American people as a whole. By leveraging this policy, a conservative administration could sideline career professionals in agencies like the Environmental Protection Agency (EPA) or Department of Justice, replacing them with individuals aligned with conservative values. This shift turns agencies into political instruments rather than impartial entities, mirroring the way authoritarian governments utilize state agencies to advance a particular ideology.

Judicial Reformation for Long-Term Control

Project 2025 also aims to secure a lasting conservative presence in the judiciary, drawing on authoritarian tactics of controlling the courts to sustain political power. Through judicial appointments and potential restructuring, Project 2025 envisions a judiciary that supports its interpretation of constitutional values, creating a legal environment that sustains conservative policies for generations. Like Hungary's Orbán, who used court reforms to cement his power, Project 2025 envisions a judiciary that will uphold its policies regardless of changing political landscapes.

Political Surveillance and Suppression

Expanding surveillance capabilities on domestic groups mirrors tactics used by authoritarian states to quell dissent. Project 2025's proposed expansion of surveillance on activists and groups that oppose its agenda takes a page from authoritarian regimes where political dissent is curtailed under the guise of national security. By framing surveillance as necessary for public safety, Project 2025 sets a precedent for monitoring and suppressing political activism, creating a chilling effect that discourages opposition.

Projecting the Potential Trajectory of the U.S. under Project 2025

The potential future trajectory of the United States under Project 2025 reflects a nation where power becomes more centralized, dissent more restricted, and democracy itself more fragile. While Project 2025 operates under the guise of "reforming" government, its proposed policies could shift American governance towards a system where the ruling administration controls the levers of power without meaningful checks or balance.

The Erosion of Democratic Institutions

Should Project 2025 succeed in implementing its policies, the nation's democratic institutions may begin to erode. The centralization of executive power, coupled with loyalty-driven hiring practices, would create federal agencies more interested in carrying out the president's vision than in upholding impartial principles. Over time, institutions like the Department of Justice or the Internal Revenue Service could become tools for rewarding allies and punishing critics, as they have been in authoritarian states. This creates a climate of distrust and fear, as people hesitate to speak out, knowing they may be targeted by a government agency.

Decline in Civil Liberties

Project 2025's focus on surveillance and policing suggests a future where Americans live under greater scrutiny, with diminished protections for privacy and freedom of speech. Laws targeting protests and surveillance on activist groups would discourage people from engaging in political expression. This trend, seen in places like Turkey and Russia, could become a reality in the United States, where political opposition is limited not only by rhetoric but also by the tangible risk of surveillance and punishment.

Altered National Identity and Global Relations

Perhaps most profoundly, a fully realized Project 2025 would redefine American identity itself. Under its agenda, American values shift from ideals of inclusion, diversity, and pluralism toward nationalism and a narrow conception of "traditional" values. The U.S. might become more insular, pulling away from global partnerships and emphasizing a nationalist agenda. The cultural and ideological shift could redefine what it means to be

American, as citizenship becomes associated with loyalty to a specific set of beliefs and policies rather than democratic values.

The lessons from authoritarian regimes around the world offer a sobering reminder of how democratic societies can fall under the sway of centralized, unchecked power. Project 2025 adapts many of these same tactics in its quest to reshape American governance. By centralizing power, controlling the judiciary, restricting opposition, and surveilling dissent, Project 2025 lays the groundwork for a nation that increasingly reflects the authoritarian regimes of history rather than the democratic republic envisioned by America's founders.

For readers concerned about the future of American democracy, understanding these historical parallels is crucial. The path Project 2025 charts is not inevitable, but its success depends on citizens remaining unaware or indifferent to the gradual erosion of democratic norms. The comparisons here, serves as a warning, a call to recognize and resist authoritarian tactics before they become entrenched. As Americans, understanding these risks is our first step toward ensuring that the country's future remains one of freedom, equality, and democracy.

CONCLUSION

As we come to the conclusion of this exploration into Project 2025, it's clear that the stakes are exceptionally high. This ambitious initiative by the Heritage Foundation and its conservative allies has outlined a vision of governance that poses substantial risks to the democratic values that form the bedrock of American society. While Project 2025 is designed to achieve stability and consistency in conservative leadership, it proposes a path that could shift the country toward a centralized, authoritarian-style government where dissent is stifled, power is heavily concentrated, and diverse voices are systematically marginalized.

Reflecting on the Risks Posed by Project 2025 to Democratic Values

At its core, Project 2025 challenges principles that Americans have come to expect from their government: transparency, accountability, separation of powers, and respect for individual freedoms. The initiative's proposals to reimagine federal agencies, restrict civil liberties, and control the judiciary all echo authoritarian strategies we've seen in regimes worldwide, from Hungary to Russia to Turkey. By concentrating authority within the executive branch, reducing the independence of federal agencies, and undermining nonpartisan governance, Project 2025 could erode the checks and balances that guard against the abuse of power.

In a Project 2025-governed America, political loyalty may increasingly become a prerequisite for public service, potentially sidelining experts and professionals who might otherwise contribute independent, unbiased perspectives. Federal agencies, once accountable to the American public, may instead become tools for advancing a narrow ideological agenda. Civil liberties, including freedom of speech and assembly, could be systematically limited under the guise of maintaining "order" and "security." Dissent, a critical ingredient of democracy, risks being branded as disruptive or even treasonous.

These changes threaten to dismantle the democratic norms that have taken centuries to develop, and, if unchecked, could make the idea of a government "by the people, for the people" a hollow phrase.

Potential Responses from Opposition Groups, Civil Society, and Global Allies

Despite the threats posed by Project 2025, there are many avenues through which democracy can be preserved and strengthened. Opposition groups, civil society, and even international allies can play critical roles in resisting authoritarianism and reinforcing democratic ideals. Each of these groups has unique resources and capabilities that can counterbalance Project 2025's ambitions.

Opposition Groups and Political Counterweights

Opposition groups within the United States have a responsibility to remain vigilant and vocal. While Project 2025 may aim to limit their influence, opposition parties, state governments, and advocacy groups can continue to educate the public on the implications of such policies. By mobilizing voters, supporting candidates committed to democratic values, and advocating for policies that uphold transparency and accountability, opposition groups can provide a political counterweight to Project 2025's agenda.

Legal challenges, too, will be essential. Courts have historically served as arbiters in preserving democratic rights, and they may yet offer avenues to challenge the constitutionality of policies that infringe upon individual freedoms or destabilize the balance of power. While Project 2025 emphasizes judicial loyalty, the judiciary, in practice, is made up of individuals who may prioritize constitutional integrity over partisanship.

Civil Society and Grassroots Mobilization

Civil society; comprising nonprofits, advocacy groups, labor unions, academic institutions, and everyday citizens, serves as the heartbeat of democracy. These groups can be incredibly effective in educating and mobilizing the public. When individuals and organizations speak out, they not only shed light on potentially harmful policies but also demonstrate that the public will not stand idly by as democratic values are undermined.

Grassroots mobilization, particularly at the local level, offers citizens a direct way to engage with issues of governance. By organizing protests, community discussions, and educational campaigns, civil society can foster a culture of awareness and resistance. Additionally, social media and digital platforms offer powerful tools for spreading awareness, rallying support, and circumventing attempts to control public narrative.

Global Allies and International Pressures

Project 2025 also risks placing the United States in a precarious position globally. Historically, the United States has championed democracy and human rights, often holding other nations accountable for authoritarian practices. Should Project 2025 move forward unchecked, it could weaken America's moral authority on the world stage, prompting concern from international allies and partners.

Countries with established democracies—such as Canada, Germany, France, and others—may become vocal critics, challenging policies that erode democracy in the United States. Global pressure can sometimes serve as a deterrent, making it politically costly for leaders to pursue authoritarian policies. Additionally, international organizations, including the United Nations, can issue statements and resolutions that highlight human rights abuses and democratic backsliding, rallying support for the preservation of American democracy.

As we've seen throughout history, the greatest defense against authoritarianism lies in the will and determination of the people. Public awareness and civic engagement are essential safeguards that keep democracy strong. While Project 2025's strategies may be meticulously designed, the ultimate power still resides with the American people. Democracy is not a static condition; it's a system that requires active participation, debate, and vigilance. If Americans remain informed, engaged, and committed to holding their leaders accountable, they can prevent the erosion of democratic institutions.

Education, transparency, and civic activism are the foundations upon which democratic resistance can be built. Schools, families, and communities must foster a culture of critical thinking and civic responsibility. Individuals who understand the mechanisms of their government are better equipped to recognize policies that undermine democracy and are more likely to act in defense of their rights.

A commitment to staying informed, voting in every election, and participating in community discussions can collectively form a bulwark against the slide toward authoritarianism. Civic engagement doesn't have to mean joining large protests or public speaking; it can be as simple as attending town hall meetings, signing petitions, or sharing information within one's network.

In the end, democracy is a shared project, a national trust that requires constant care and vigilance. As Americans, it is our responsibility to defend this trust, to protect it for future generations, and to ensure that government remains a reflection of our diverse, pluralistic society. Project 2025 may represent a conservative vision for governance, but the choice between authoritarianism and democracy lies squarely with the people.

America's democratic experiment has endured for centuries not because of any single leader or ideology, but because of a collective commitment to liberty, justice, and equality. As we look ahead, let's remember that democracy, though fragile, is resilient when its citizens are steadfast in its defense.